DESERT RETREATS

DESERT RETREATS
SEDONA STYLE

LINDA LEIGH PAUL

photography by **MICHAEL MATHERS**

UNIVERSE

First published in the United States of America in 2003 by

UNIVERSE PUBLISHING

A Division of Rizzoli International Publications, Inc.

300 Park Avenue South

New York, NY 10010

www.rizzoliusa.com

2003   2004   2005   2006   2007   /   10   9   8   7   6   5   4   3   2   1

PAGE ii: The Color of Air. *George Stocking Photography. All rights reserved.*

DESIGNED BY SARA E. STEMEN

PRINTED IN HONG KONG

ISBN: 0-7893-0983-1

LIBRARY OF CONGRESS CONTROL NUMBER: 2003104736

CONTENTS

ABOUT DESERTS I COULD WRITE that people die every day for a lack of knowledge about what is found there. This echo of William Carlos Williams rings true when many worlds are revealed through the contemplation of a simple object. Imagine the rewards of one glimpse at the vastness of the desert, one stone *left unturned;* a universe filled with the simplest things. For the rewards I have encountered, I am grateful indeed to those who have loved and love Arizona.

I wish to express my appreciation especially to Michael Quinn of the Grand Canyon National Parks Museum Collection; Sue Grinols of the Fine Arts Museum of San Francisco; Margo Stipe, curator of the Frank Lloyd Wright Archives at Taliesin West; Edith Denton and Kathie Hamblen of the Sedona Historical Society; Erica Stoller of Esto; Pamela Quick, rights and permissions manager at MIT Press; Pamela Johnson of the Dorothea Tanning Studio in New York; and to Marilyn Booth-Love for her passion for decorum, history, and escapade.

I am again indebted to Peter Belluschi for his enthusiasms and the good will with which he contributes his knowledge, resources, and time. Thank you, Peter, for introducing me to the idea and the reality of Sedona. An outstanding part of that reality was the privilege of meeting Peter's colleague, architect Charlie van Block, whose thoughts about architecture are just what architecture is all about: sheer, joyous existence. I would like to thank the Sedona homeowners who graciously opened their homes to us and the architects who shared their time. My thanks go particularly to Jennifer Aderhold for her many talents and her ability to put more hours in a day than God ever intended, and to her colleagues,

Max Licher and Mike Bower of Design Group Architects. For superb Sedona hospitality, I would like to thank Jennifer Combs of the Sedona–Oak Creek Chamber of Commerce; June Jochum of J. B. Jochum and Associates; Karon Cullen and the management at L'Auberge de Sedona. Their generosity made my visits unforgettable. The entire project was made memorable by photographer Michael Mathers and his special humor about how to get things done. Well done.

I wish to express my profound admiration and respect for Alexandra Tart, senior editor at Rizzoli / Universe; she has the spirit of the Morning Star and the presence of the Evening Star—brilliant and unwavering. I am thoroughly grateful for her commitment to this book from its inception to its completion. It is my wish that the stars continue to align for Charles Miers, Rizzoli/Universe's extraordinary publisher.

This book was written during my mental conversations with John Van Dyke, Mary Hunter Austin, Edward Abbey, and Max Ernst, who make me laugh joyfully and cry. It is also for R. Carlos Nakai, whose sweet cedar flute notes found me and told me of this mythological place; and Will Bruder of Will Bruder Architects, Ltd., who told me—and not in vain—that there is a modern sacred ground in Sedona.

I would like to dedicate this book to Dorothea Tanning of New York, for her seventy years of painting, poetry, and sculpture, and for her pure love of Sedona. Thank you, Ms. Tanning, for the treasures you have given us all.

Robert Paul, critic and partner, is a marvel of humor and love.

OPPOSITE: *Sinaqua culture petroglyph, Coconino National Forest, near Sedona, AZ.*

THE ROAD TO SEDONA is a pilgrimage. One of the mysteries in this part of the world is *Hay-A-Pa-O*, a Hopi phrase of reverence for "the forces of the air." *Hay-A-Pa-O* keep the legends of the Speaker Chief and of all North American First Speakers flowing in and along canyon walls and the fractured towers that are found here. The land and skyscapes, designed by wind and water, are a fleeting realm between nature and culture. They are the daughters of *Hay-A-Pa-O*. How important is air in this ancient and modern landscape? It is the all-consuming inexplicable; it constitutes Life in the southwest desert. The powers are found in the forms of the sun, the mountains, and the thunder clouds, as well as in colors—yellow shows the way north; red indicates the south; white portends the east; and turquoise blue signifies the enchantment of the west.

If there is a place on earth to explore free will, it is in Sedona, Arizona. Every pilgrimage begins a journey of the heart, an opening of the soul, and a sharpening of the mind and body. On this irreversible venture toward personal inner sancta, we necessarily shed all human constraints and reclaim the power of infinite choice. Sedona is an examination of the good life. Its architecture embodies the ancient argument between the philosophers and the poets about the nature of human life and how to live it. Here we learn that architectural choices are moral choices that show our reverence for life. Sedona's architectural influences are unique and exciting. The surrounding ancient architecture begets the reinterpreted work of Mary Colter, as well as the pinnacle of modern architecture, the work of Frank Lloyd Wright. For centuries, to the north, south, east, and west of Sedona, spores of this architectural history lay upon the earth. And now, these rich inheritances have given rise to today's new indigenous Arizona architecture.

The houses featured in this book are spirited entities. They are as much artifacts of human effort and workmanship as are the treasures of the great chieftains. They are the legacy of modern genius; those who design and live in them show us how to live a modern yet deliberate life. Each household in this book incorporates two of the owners' passions: the house itself, and its owners' personal inner mystique; art, animals, athletics, aesthet-

OPPOSITE: *Maidenhair fern growing out of a seep in a Supai formation, Red Rock Secret Mountain Wilderness area, west of Sedona.*

ics, meditation, or healing. Here in Sedona, where culture is artifice and nature reigns, the ideal activity brings the two into harmony; this is the purpose of architecture, the *action* of it.

Two forces are at work in architecture: the creative process, which asks questions, and the design process, which answers them. A persistent question surrounding the ancient sites near Sedona is: to what extent does the Anasazi architecture have a bearing on today's world? V. B. Price replies, "it is not our way to design great houses along a cosmological scheme that creates a sacred calendar out of a built environment."[1] However, it might be a tremendous advantage to do so. Price suggests that today's architects could devise a new strategy to identify the concepts of neighborliness, self-help, and democracy. It is an idea that has been touched upon, but as yet, is still seen as a concept that only *seems* like a good idea.

An aboriginal attraction to unadorned loveliness is the true lure of Sedona. It lies in the eye of what writer Mary Hunter Austin called "the country of lost borders,"[2] where the ethereal and the elusive become the genius loci. Natural space, that is, the great geometries of the earth, make Sedona blossom as an essential force that drifts into surrounding forests, beside shallow creeks, and upward among valiant buttes. It is a land occulted by ancient narratives entwined with unseen powers—rising on eddies of air that seek to connect the earth with the sky.

One hundred years ago, this Arizona breath and myth was championed as a national treasure by Mary Austin, who wrote, "There is the divinest, cleanest air to be breathed anywhere in God's world. Someday the world will understand that."[3] A fervent and vocal environmentalist, Austin believed that the day would come when Americans would honor their desert air. In this regard, Sedona surpasses the ideal of romanticism and sails into the province of the oracle.

Sedona is a land of revelation and uncommon remembrances. The aesthete wanderer Professor John Van Dyke walked across the southwestern desert's benches, canyons, and mesas in 1898. He traversed the land with his fox terrier, Cappy, and a western-bred pony, the only pony dependable on the rocky, dry trails. His impressions of that territory were engraved on his heart and in his mind when he later wrote, "Life becomes simplified from necessity. It begins all over again starting at the primitive stage. . . . Civilization, the race, history, philosophy, art—how very far away and how very useless, even contemptible . . . they seem."[4] A professor of art history at Rutgers, Van Dyke had spent most of his life in the finest galleries of Europe. Now, however, for almost three

OPPOSITE: *The Forces of the Air.*

years he devoted his attention to the colors and sounds of the earth, air, and sky. Alone, he *heard* each rise and retreat of the ancient waters, underground channels, and pools; of shallow beaches, bays, and shorelines; of rippling waves and spray; and of evaporation, wind, and land forms becoming lost in *Hay-A-Pa-O*. Van Dyke heard the rivers that once flowed north change their direction; he heard the circling winds form buttes and mesas, and he fell in love with what he perceived as the most enigmatic landscape in the world. He wrote, "The great struggle of the painter is to get on with the least possible form and to suggest everything by tones of color, shades of light and drifts of air."[5] He believed that his greatest knowledge came from the euphoria of his experience; only as a lover of the desert could he learn. At the center of Van Dyke's trek through a land that he believed would be best served by the aesthetic sense rather than corporeal needs, is Sedona, a surreal dream.

In the land around Sedona, the idea of "human scale" seems not relevant. The magnitude of the surrounding geology is never viewed as being *in proportion* to humankind. In a world where humans once used stone partitions to mortar their work spaces and crop harvests into small, eccentric cervices in the sides of Promethean cliff walls, *scale* becomes a matter of fashioning oneself to the landscape. Sedona architecture is a remedy, a means of soothing and healing. It is a haven and a gathering place for those who honor the earth above all else.

One of the architects represented in this book makes a habit of camping on a site as part of his design process. Once he camped at a site for years before he began to design the house. During the weeks of construction, he slept on open floors, watching the night and the stars while the framing went up around him. Finally, the time came to shut out his sky with a roof, and suddenly the design changed. He knew the stars and satellites and the color of midnight far too well to lose them to a roof with no opportunity to view the night sky.

OPPOSITE: *A Palatki ruin of a Sinagua culture cliff dwelling, Coconino National Forest, near Sedona.*

PART ONE

ARCHITECTURE PURE AND SIMPLE

Remember, the past is where you are going.

ANONYMOUS

When architecture is simple and pure, it is sometimes seen as primitive, crude, or undeveloped. Yet even after we have absorbed thousands of years of architectural styles, trends, and periods, we find that purity and simplicity continue to persevere as principles of design. If, as Ezra Pound says, poetry is the most compressed form of verbal expression, then perhaps the most compressed form of design is architecture pure and simple.

THE INTIMATE, ONE-ROOM RETREATS we relish—the writer's hut, the tea house, and the Swedish *lusthus*—are a flowering of the primitive hut, the first aboriginal shelter. Small, compact, and part of the wilderness, the primitive hut is a touchstone for our ideas about architecture. Although we do not honor a particular chief or priest for this first creation, we do have a story. In the mythical beginning, as supposed by French architect and theorist Eugène Emmanuel Viollet-le-Duc, was the fictional metaphysical being, *Epergos*. First, *Epergos* teaches early humans to build a shelter by searching out tender saplings that grow close to each other in a somewhat circular pattern. Next, *Epergos* shows them how to tie the highest part of the branches together to create an inverted cone shape. He teaches them to braid the young saplings together, cover them with mud, and use a mixture of dirt and mud for a solid floor. In Viollet-le-Duc's view, the habitations were too unhewn to be considered "architecture," as they were minimally functional and required no refinement of materials. Most important, they did not display any of the moral values often associated with true architecture. Today, however, our one-room retreats, as well as all architecture, are often viewed as refuges with a "moral" purpose.

The first building after Viollet-le-Duc.

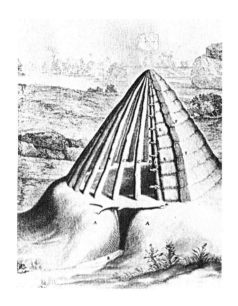

THE CONE SHAPE OF THE PRIMITIVE HUT was given to humans not by *Epergos*, but by Nature herself. The huts begin to appear in northeastern Europe around 25,000 years ago. Available twigs and mud allowed for swift construction; thus, the form followed human migration from Asia Minor to Siberia, to Western North America, then southward where it insinuated itself into what is now the American Southwest. The early North Americans who built and settled semi-permanent sites were an early branch of an archaic 6,000-year-old "desert culture," later known to us as the Anasazi. In Navajo culture, the word varies in meaning with intonation. One inflection means, "ancient people who are not us."

The first Anasazi dwellings were like the primitive hut, although they evolved into more stable pit houses. Earth was excavated to a depth of one to three feet, and the conical shape remained above ground. The structure was covered with a layer of mud for insulation. The earthen half-walls retained heat from the fire and the shelter was a relatively efficient structure. In time, four upright posts and several lateral posts were fashioned into a frame above the excavation. The framing was overlaid with *lattia*, a wall of small sticks latticed with branches, which formed a flat roof and sloping walls. An entrance through the roof is the first sign of the traditional *kiva*, the ceremonial gathering place intrinsic to Anasazi life and ritual.

LEFT: *A conical reconstruction by Claude Perrault.*

RIGHT: *A reconstructed pit house of the Anasazi culture.*

The Spruce Tree House terrace with ladders and rooftop entrances to kivas. Built between 1200 and 1276 A.D. *, it had 114 rooms and 8 kivas.*

The Spruce Tree House kiva with ladder and reconstructed ceiling, occupied in the twelfth and thirteenth centuries.

THE INDIGENOUS AMERICAN ARCHITECTURE is the Anasazi constructs of the Southwest. How did the first builders learn to cut and stack stones in a straight line, or leave holes for windows, view points, and ventilation pathways? Was the use of long wooden beams or large flat rocks in building construction accidental or calculated? The Anasazi were, of course, surrounded by thousands of strata of rock, era upon era. Horizontal and vertical lines fashioned their lives, their calendars, and their location in the desert. During nomadic raids on their crops, the people moved from pit houses on the sloping sides of canyons, in the rolling desert, and alongside the flat mesas to nearby caves in the cliffs in their stone-walled landscape. They built stone and rock buildings that partitioned the deep caves in the back from the kiva and walled rooms in the front, which then *became* the landscape. These temporary cliff dwellings and towers were very difficult to reach, even for the Anasazi themselves, and nearly impregnable to their enemies. Great inconvenience, though, meant little to people driven by fear. In their cliff sites they were protected from every direction, except the front, where they commanded a full view of an approach. When the days of the raids passed, the people may have begun to move out of the cliffs to build again on mesas, and in the rusted canyons, green valleys, and yellow deserts, where the demands of terrain invoked free-standing design.

A desert building should be notably simple in outline as the region itself is sculptured: should have learned from the cactus many secrets of straight-line-patterns for its forms, playing with the light and softening the building into its proper place among the organic desert creations—We do not yet understand such pattern in form because it is an attribute of a very high and perhaps older Culture. —Frank Lloyd Wright[6]

ARIZONA HAS AN UNPARALLELED architectural heritage. When the time arrived for America's larger-than-life architect to encounter the desert, he became enchanted with its possibilities. South of Sedona, Wright's dream for Taliesin West emerged from the rocky floor under the sun, using the same orderliness and methods that the Anasazi used to select materials and build on their sites. Wright enthusiasts, however, claim that no influences of the indigenous desert architecture are apparent at Taliesin West. Arata Isozaki writes:

> *. . . any attempt to discuss Wright's space in terms of its multifarious historical and cultural antecedents is doomed to failure, for their vestiges, exemplified by Wright's reworking of Lao-tzu's fundamental principle, are rephrased and irretrievably buried in every aspect of his work. . . . The incomparably individual process of Wright's work is the unprejudiced incorporation of the legacy of every civilization, of Whitman and Lao-tzu, of Aztec and Momoyama Japanese.[7]*

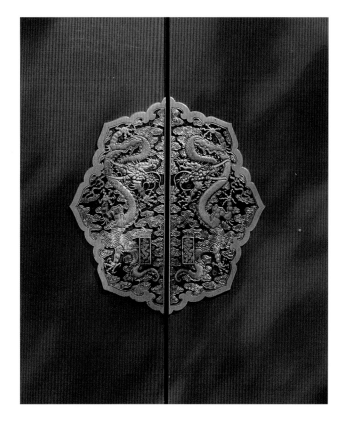

ABOVE: *Dragon pieces from Frank Lloyd Wright's collection of Asian art appear on the cabaret doors at Taliesin West.*

OPPOSITE: *The hall with Frank Lloyd Wright in the drafting room at right. Oranges cool in the corner.*

*The Bell Tower at
Taliesin West (1951).*

Frank Lloyd Wright's study (1951) at Taliesin West.

Nevertheless, many evident references and principles similar to the architecture of America's First Speakers can be found in Wright's own fundamental spatial work. This primary principle is clearly addressed in this example by Neil Levine:

> *What is much more significant are the spaces between and around the buildings—the walkways, bridges, platforms and terraces that not only connect building to building but link the entire complex to the mountains and valley surrounding it and to the prehistoric usages associated with them.*[8]

This is an accurate description of the cliff dwellings at Spruce Tree House and other sites. Wright envisioned Taliesin atop a vast mesa above the Salt-Gila River Valley. His apprentices gathered tons of multicolored volcanic rock from Taliesin's vast acreage, mixed it with cement, combined it with redwood, and continued the desert prophecy of terraces, parapets, walls, and steps. The rock and concrete mixture, known as Wright's famed *desert masonry*, was cast into flat, stepped, and angled forms. Poured in place, the masonry created massive layers, which are the Taliesin walls, hallways, seating, terraces, steps, structural piers, and sculpture. Taliesin's interior spaces have been described as *cave-like*, and Wright was proud to include a kiva. Upon the completion of Taliesin West, Olgivanna Wright said, "The whole opus looked like something they had been excavating." Wright agreed:

> *That desert camp belonged to the desert as though it had stood there for centuries. . . . Taliesin West had its own desert playhouse: a kiva of solid masonry, inside and out, with a sunken fireplace . . . a triumph of imagination by way of simple form and limited space in the heart of a great cubical masonry block.*[9]

Wright believed that the early southwest builders had *nothing* of the desert in their architecture. He claimed, in fact, "[a]rchitecture, *the great art*, except in very primitive terms, was beyond" them.[10]

It is true that Wright built a magnificent desert shrine to his concepts of space and form, yet he eschewed the genius of Anasazi architecture. As a result, his contradictions are as glaring as the desert floor. It was a miscalculation for Wright to claim that the "great art" of architecture was "beyond" the Anasazi. Wright raked the desert floor for building materials, as did the Anasazi. Wright sited his compound according to the direction of the afternoon and setting sun, as was Anasazi practice. Wright incorporated the concept of the kiva into Taliesin West, a space and use invented by the Anasazi; and again, Wright's use of open space around and between the enclosed spaces is nearly identical to that found at Anasazi sites. Anasazi constructs may have been a more valuable form of that greater art than Wright himself could have imagined. Anasazi architecture gives us their language: a way to understand astronomy, to remember mathematics, and to preserve nature in its purest form.

By merely pushing out walls and incorporating angular features, interior supports, exaggerated forms, pools of water, and the greatest ally of the modernists, glass, Wright was able to turn the primitive and beautiful of the desert into the luxurious.

The pool, Madonna stone, bridge, and water tower at the east end of Pergola (1951).

The pool and drafting room from the south (1951).

Mary Colter's Watchtower at Desert View.

WATCHTOWER AT DESERT VIEW

architect: **MARY ELIZABETH JANE COLTER**

"... it is of the earth, not the sky, yet it is the first star of the Morning."
—Arnold Berke[11]

WHEN FRANK LLOYD WRIGHT began digging rocks from the desert and planning Taliesin West south of Sedona, Mary Elizabeth Jane Colter was in her thirty-fifth year of creating architecture in and of the desert. North of Sedona, she began drawings for the Watchtower at Desert View at the Grand Canyon in 1931. Colter loved the rugged Arizona landscape and was fascinated by the odd details that she often found when exploring the sites of indigenous architecture. She believed that the ancient landmarks and the cultural heritage of the Southwest were a prayer. Her respect for the forms, materials, patterns, etchings, and designs—the oddities that she called "erratic tricks"—found at these sites was her architectural guide. More than conceptual touchstones, the beauty and integrity of the Anasazi architecture led her to re-create one of the predominant forms found in the region, the tower. She chose to honor the round form with the Watchtower at Desert View. Colter recognized that once the circular form is mastered, it is the easiest and strongest shape to build. Circular masonry was well known among the First Speakers of the American Southwest. In these ancient cultures the tower evolved from the round excavated foundations of the pit houses. Some pit houses were found to have incorporated flat stone floors and stone walls, and are believed to be some of the earliest below-grade stone foundations. Colter thought that curved tower walls withstood the elements far better that any

other form. She claimed that architectural ruins of the D-shaped buildings, including taller towers, proved that flat walls fell first while curved walls were left standing. There were many examples of square watch towers, too. One interesting theory of the towers is that they were designed for astronomical observation. The archeologist J. Walter Fewkes thought the towers were sun houses or observatories. They were, he believed, used by high priests to coordinate solar movements and to record points of the rising and setting sun. Here the priests could create their planting calendars, worship the sun, and pray to *Hay-A-Pa-O*.

Colter left a cultural insignia in her buildings at the Grand Canyon—at Phantom Ranch, Hopi House, Bright Angel Lodge, Lookout Studio, and Hermit's Rest. She had planned to build her retirement home on ten acres of land that she had purchased many years before in Sedona. She was, though, a woman who worked as long as there was work to do, and when her retirement did arrive, it was much later than she had planned. Sedona was still a remote place in 1947, and although Mary loved the red rock country, she chose to retire in Santa Fe, where many of her friends from her Grand Canyon days lived. She sold her parcel of land in Sedona to a couple named Jack and Helen Frye, and Mary Colter's land became part of the almost mythical Smoke Trail Ranch.[12]

The round tower built on a boulder at Hovenweep.

The round tower at Mesa Verde's Cliff Palace.

A square tower set into boulders.

Colter's Lookout Studio was built as a daring outcrop of the canyon edge.

House of Apache Fire on the Smoke Trail Ranch.

HOUSE OF APACHE FIRE

JACK AND HELEN FRYE

TOP: *Helen Frye at Smoke Trail Ranch.*

BOTTOM: *The House of Apache Fire terrace and desert.*

ONE OF SEDONA'S MOST UNFORGETTABLE visual arts and curative arts pioneers was Helen Frye. Helen moved to Sedona with her husband Jack, then president of a fledgling airline, TWA, with Howard Hughes. As Helen and Jack flew over the rocky red Sedona landscape in 1941, Helen saw luminous clouds rising from the rock forms below like tiny vortices. Instinctively, Helen knew that below her was the precise spot where she was destined to build her house and to live. They found the very rocks they had flown over and, along with Mary Colter's parcel, the land became known as the Smoke Trail Ranch.

On her way to the ranch the road was very crooked. It reminded Helen of smoke rising from a fire; the way it twisted and turned all the way to her house. A woman of unusual beauty, Helen was also a woman with a past. She had been married to a Vanderbilt and was devoted to art, healing, medicine, and meditation, with a strong belief in reincarnation. In 1948, once again single, she built a studio for herself on the ranch. It was built using the local red rock on an outcropping above the creek. As the legend goes, during the construction Yavapai-Apache builders lived on her land during the long work week. Bunk houses were available, but this group preferred sleeping under the stars, near their campfires, near the water. In the early night blue, the fires could be seen from a distance as their smoke drifted far out over the ranch. The studio became known thereafter as the House of Apache Fire. Helen personified the holistic life. She inspired the human spirit and set the pace as the cultural exemplar of Sedona.

THE KITTREDGES

IN 1930 BOB KITTREDGE roared through Sedona and into Oak Creek Canyon on a Harley Davidson, one of the first ever built. Attached was a sidecar carrying his brother, a pet monkey, and an orphaned coyote pup. The two Kittredge brothers had a long-lasting dream of creating a bastion in the woods, and in Sedona land was only sixty dollars an acre. They began building the first cottage, Log House, which took three years to complete. More cabins were built one by one until the fifteenth—and last—one was completed more than fifty years later.

Bob and his wife, Mary, were sculptors. When they weren't clearing land and building, Bob cast western bronze sculptures and Mary carved African mahogany or painted. In 1946 they built their studio. All of the Forest Houses have the power to refresh and inspire, but the studio is a working space. The front door opens into a large room with a small kitchen on the right. To the left a staircase leads to the loft. Skylights fill half the ceiling and large rolling warehouse doors open for lifting large pieces in or out of the studio.

In the 1940s, the Kittredges became close friends of the surrealists Dorothea Tanning and Max Ernst when they arrived in Sedona. Max and Bob were tremendous friends and worked closely together to build Rock House in 1946, which was the first cabin designed to be a rental. Tanning described Bob Kittredge as "an Atlas of a man" and their compound as an "earthly paradise in Oak Creek Canyon . . . a beautiful, rather savage setting: a rushing stream, high pines and red cliff."[13] The studio was a gathering place for world-traveling artists, as well as those artists who visited and settled in Sedona. Today there are fifteen extraordinary cabins at Forest Houses, each as warm and remote as ever.

ABOVE: *A Diamond House bedroom lamp light in the woods*

OPPOSITE: *Trout House rises from the creek and the rocks.*

Bob and Mary Kittredge's studio, built in 1946.

ABOVE:

Bob Kittredge sledding logs in winter to build a cabin.

NEAR RIGHT:

Bob Kittredge and the Harley Davidson he rode into Oak Creek Canyon, circa 1930.

FAR RIGHT:

Mary Kittredge relaxes on cabin framing.

RIGHT:

Bob Kittredge designed and created a molded plywood kitchen counter and a curved stairway to the loft.

OPPOSITE:

The studio with skylights and large rolling doors for moving heavy pieces in and out. Stairs to the loft are on the left.

OPPOSITE: *Rock House, built by Bob Kittredge and Max Ernst in 1946.*

BELOW: *Stone cabin above Oak Creek.*

Dorothea Tanning, Max Ernst, and a neighbor building their house in Sedona in 1946.

CAPRICORN HILL

MAX ERNST AND DOROTHEA TANNING

UPON VIEWING THE SEDONA LANDSCAPE on his first visit, the German surrealist painter Max Ernst was overcome with bewilderment. Before him stretched his own imagination: the landscapes and images he had been painting for years before ever visiting the United States. As a leader of a movement that expressed the necessity of freedom from the confines of a rational life, Ernst believed that society curtailed the supernatural aspects of one's individual spirit; his *discovery* of Sedona matched his artistic ideals and presented him and his fellow artists with a boundless spiritual universe.

Ernst and his brilliant wife, Dorothea Tanning, bought a spectacular piece of land in Sedona in 1946. Their presence in Sedona brought avant-garde literary and artistic thought to an area steeped in desert lore. Most important, their presence, along with the likes of Helen Frye, the Kittredges, and others, helped cultivate Sedona's affinity for the international art world.

Ernst, Tanning, and friends built a small, unexceptional house with no electricity: a kitchen, a screened sleeping porch, and Dorothea's studio. Ernst built his own studio near the house. One day Dorothea said, "This is Capricorn Hill." For eight years they lived and worked in a landscape that insinuated itself into their lives and their art. In 2001, Tanning wrote:

> You would think that here ends the story, that those velvet nights, preludes to each passionate day in a landscape so charged that "if Wagner had seen this his music would be louder than it is already" (someone was saying), were more than enough. Did not this paradise firmly hold us in thrall, sustain us hilariously in our ongoing combat with need, the creature kind, and provide the sweep of background—a long luminous brushstroke upon which to pin, plaster, and paint our questions and our answers for the rest of our lives?[14]

Painting in the desert was difficult: "The heat was so intense, so aged . . . big gestures such as covering a canvas with quick paint were reserved for evenings . . . when five o'clock saw the sun dip behind our hill and . . . the temperature dropped twenty degrees."[15]

Ernst and Tanning encouraged their New York circle and others to escape the city and enjoy a cool reinvigorating stop at the Kittredges' rustic cabins. Friends Henri Cartier-Bresson, Vladimir Nabokov, Dylan Thomas, Charles Henri Ford, Marcel Duchamp, and Man Ray were a few of those who stopped to visit during the Ernst and Tanning period in Sedona. A crossroads and a gathering place, Capricorn Hill was filled with the work of their circle of New York and European friends, the great art of the era. Theirs was an extraordinary collection of sculpture, paintings, and photographs.

Faith Fuller, a Sedona resident and friend of Ernst and Tanning, tells a story about the day Frank Lloyd Wright came from Taliesin to Sedona. He arrived at Capricorn Hill dressed in suit and hat, knocked on the door, and told the housekeeper that he was there to see the house. Wright was informed that the Ernsts were in France and that he could *not* see the house. "I am Frank Lloyd Wright and I want to see this house!" he demanded. The housekeeper replied, "I am Edie Randall and you won't!" Wright had actually come to view the art, not the house, but he did not see either. The legacy of Ernst and Tanning in Sedona is an appreciation for work, land, and the freedom of the spirit. It is a dedication to all art forms, particularly painting and sculpture.

70/75

max ernst

LEFT:

Max Ernst, French (born Germany),
1891–1976. Paysage Arizona, *1960.*
Color Etching.

OPPOSITE:

Dorothea Tanning and Max Ernst
with Capricorn *in Sedona, 1946.*

Dorothea and Max's three-room Sedona house, with a Kwakiutl totem at the entrance, 1947.

Dorothea Tanning, 1910–present. Self-Portrait, 1944. Oil on canvas.

PART TWO

ARCHITECTURAL ALCHEMY

In that camera-sharp place where the only electricity was in such thunderous lightning,
there were no sounds in the afternoon save the hum of the heat. It was so intense, so lurking,
so aged, that we the intruders felt also quiet, intense, and strangely on tiptoe, as if in peril.
The heat bounced like coiled springs off the burning red rocks and melted the tar on our
paper roof. It came inside to sit on my eyes. Breathing was important, an event.

DOROTHEA TANNING
Between Lives

There are countless descriptions of the red rock desert, but there is something about it that is always just beyond the reach of words, something inexpressible. People who build houses there are affected by this inexpressible presence and create what they could never have imagined in any other place on earth. They experience the transforming energy of the desert, of light and dark, lightning and thunder, angles and spires, rocks and timbers, sticks and water, and the living powers of the air.

WICKIUP HOUSE

owner: **SUZAN ANN MAGAZINER**

architects: **PIERCE & PIERCE ARCHITECTS**

FEW HOUSES IN SEDONA radiate the elegant authenticity of their era, as does this extraordinary 1970s design by Walter S. Pierce of Boston. The design was commissioned by Dorothy and Randolph Compton, Suzan Magaziner's grandparents, who were drawn to Sedona as a place where they could share their love of airplanes, rocks, art, and cameras with artists in Sedona's growing creative community.

The house was planned as a vacation gathering place for a large and dispersed family. Designed as an assemblage of separate wings around a central covered atrium, four buildings house a main living, dining, and kitchen unit as well as sleeping quarters, a housekeeping unit, and a combination rock-polishing shop and bunk house for the grandchildren. The stylistic and conceptual plans were influenced by Wrightian Usonian styles, and included the Taliesin West motif of Wright's desert masonry. The floors of the house are the classic California pigmented concrete and rival the best concrete work of the day.

The character of the house speaks of the best of modern architectural intentions, inviting visitors to linger. The sleek sophistication of the broad spaces and subtle elevation changes are combined with natural oak and ash finishes on furniture and cabinetry throughout the house. The Comptons furnished the house with the work of the Indians of the Southwest. Rugs and blankets are used on walls and floors; the desert masonry walls are ideal for niches that can hold baskets and ceramic pieces. Interior finishes and trim are a rough-sawn redwood, left unfinished.

As a teenager, Suzan Magaziner visited the house during school breaks and pitched in when the desert masonry walls went up. There, among the piñon pines, Arizona cypress, and a few impertinent cacti, Suzan explored the canyons and ruins of Sedona. Many residential sites in Sedona are built on land bearing pot shards and occasionally a nearly intact artifact, reminding us that the ancient clans were all over this land. For Suzan, stumbling upon ruins in the red rock wilderness of Sedona meant confessing to her own reverential silences. Sedona meant building, carefully and deliberately.

Many of Suzan's early Sedona remembrances germinated and now flourish in her unique creative life as seen in Suzan's Light House (see page 129). Today the Wickiup House is back to an almost original clean and spartan perfection. The restoration has been a labor of love for Suzan and her architect, Paul Froncek. If society does not cherish the architecture of the past, what will become of us? Without our past, how do we know who we are?

The delicate planes of early Sedona modernism quietly charm the landscape.

Breezes cool as they circulate around desert masonry walls.

The dining room steps down to the sunken living room, which features casual furnishings and a built-in upholstered sofa.

The scale of the boulders in the wall emphasizes the length of the sofa and counterbalances the interior accessories. Max Ernst paintings hang above the sofa.

LEFT: *Overhead spotlighting creates a gallery entrance.*

RIGHT: *The lovely covered and uncovered atria connect to each wing of the house.*

LEFT:
*One of many small, quiet areas
for reading or relaxing.*

OPPOSITE:
*The vistas surround the house
with peace and beauty.*

owners: **STAN AND ROSANNE CROOKE**

architects: **DESIGN GROUP ARCHITECTS**

OVERLOOKING DESERT SCRUB, washes, and an occasional javelina sits a sublime house of a contemporary design. Enigmatic as the pyramids, it expands and spreads in intervals of volume and light, strength and fragility. Exterior forms are used to create unions of opposites designed for balance. Architect Mike Bower attributes the strength to "a palette of forms"—flat frontal facades, broad horizontal lines in the courtyard, and deep inset floor-to-ceiling windows accentuate the variety of forms. Solid geometry is offset by the delicate patterns of sandstone tile cladding. The exterior forms flow, quite unexpectedly, into a monument of stability and lofty lightness.

A copper gate at the front entry bears a pattern of diminishing cubes. This motif is mirrored in a triptych sconce and window as well as throughout the architecture. The gate opens to reveal a sedate Zen courtyard of raked rocks with a large stone bench and water feature. The tiny rocks are a counterpoint to the magnitude of the buttes in the distance. A cool breeze circulates around the *corrédor* that encompasses the rock garden, a rare object of contemplation in Sedona.

OPPOSITE: *The pool is as sacrosanct as a halo in the high desert.*

RIGHT: *The geometries of design and materials amplify the surrounding land formations.*

Maple cabinetry, bookcases, and credenzas fill rooms with crisp, yet tactile surfaces. In the study, maple paneling disguises media centers and cabinets in the wall cladding. In a bedroom, the headboard of the bed and built-in cabinets are made of the ever present, sensual maple. In the kitchen, maple woodwork is trimmed with cherrywood. The living room, too, is finished in travertine and cherrywood with maple. Overhead, in every room, the chamfered ceilings are illuminated with soft recessed lighting and maple panels with cherry insets.

Bower's partner, Max Licher, explains that the composition of the house is a series of small forms; a repetition of patterns and forms. It is the sort of *pattern in form* to which Frank Lloyd Wright referred, one that gains strength because of its "system of economy," that is, its shared segments. When these forms are put into the hands of masterful architects, spaces become intriguing in their complexity and remain genius in their simplicity.

TOP LEFT:

The private study is designed for respite. The furnishings of work and entertainment are concealed behind panels of maple cabinetry.

BOTTOM LEFT:

Brushed stainless steel torchieres frame the entrance to the living room. The entry table was designed by Jennifer Aderhold.

OPPOSITE:

Dining room furnishings offer subtle luxury. The view, however, remains the focus.

The architects fused palettes and patterns to create strength and fragility in the design.

LEFT: *A copper entry gate opens onto the Zen mediation garden, with a single large boulder bench and waterfall.*

RIGHT: *The warmth of simplicity and light.*

HOUSE OF TWO BRIDGES

architect: **GORDON ROGERS ARCHITECT, INC., A.I.A.**

A CLIENT'S REQUEST FOR SIMPLICITY, grace, and interesting roof lines—all on one floor—without the use of right angles, inspired this breathtaking design. On 3.2 acres, divided by a fast running arroyo, architect Gordon Rogers designed a masterpiece with three individual buildings and two bridges to accommodate the extraordinary rocky beauty of the site. Each building is defined by a gently curving copper roof plane. From the underside of the roof, the ceilings are a soft sweep of rough-hewn cedar planks, which add a spectacular clerestory above the traditional wall height.

The approach to the house is through a gate and crosses a bridge over the arroyo to a wide set of steps. The steps lead to a glass wall and the main door, around the corner. The door opens into the foyer, where a stone wall separates the foyer from the kitchen. To the right is the great room. There, the pigmented concrete floor and soft, soaring ceiling are connected by a magnificent red rock wall and fireplace treatment. The great room includes a conversation area near the fireplace and a second lounge space, the dining area, an informal bar, and

OPPOSITE: *The rusted steel footbridge leads to the entrance.*

RIGHT: *The entrance features whitewashed cedar on the ceiling and the California red–pigmented concrete floor. The feather-wing motif in copper appears on the front door. The bronze sculpture is by Ken Payne.*

the kitchen. This is largest of the three structures, which are connected by an enclosed bridge that doubles as a hall and gallery, connecting the kitchen to the building that houses a study. The third structure is the guest quarters, or in the parlance of the owners, the "bunk house."

As a complement to the owners' collection of western bronzes and paintings, Jennifer Aderhold designed contemporary furnishings for each room, with an expert eye for form and pattern. The red rock, burnishing copper, and rusted steel hues demanded Jennifer's expertise when it came to selecting pattern, tone, and shape for interior pieces. The result is orchestral beauty among the red rocks.

The three separate "entities" of the house are connected by two bridges and set lightly in the wilderness.

The low profile of the main structure features the truss system. It begins low at the entry level and curves gently upward to a height of twenty-two feet. It was a very economical and fast design solution that allowed expansive red rock vistas.

LEFT:
*The sensual swell of the curved
truss, angles of reflecting glass,
and landscaping are nearly a
camouflage.*

OPPOSITE:
*All interior furnishings were
designed by Jennifer Aderhold to
complement the owners' bronze
Western art.*

PATTERSON RESIDENCE

owners: **BOB AND CLAUDIA PATTERSON**

architects: **DESIGN GROUP ARCHITECTS**

THE PATTERSONS WERE CERTAIN about one thing when they began designing their new home in Sedona: they wanted to avoid the typical geometries of building and come up with a design that expressed a tender, soft feeling. Many conversations with the architects soon transformed early drawings into a subtle flow of line and form around a central kiva. The owners wanted a feeling that the house itself was "embracing" the people in it. "We wanted rounded walls and gentle curves. We continued talking and planning until the warmth of the design was perceptible on the page," said Claudia.

The Pattersons moved to Sedona to put down roots in a small community where they could be involved in its many community activities. They gain "peace and inner strength" from the variations of the four mild seasons in Sedona and from the lordly red rocks themselves.

When planning the materials of the house, the couple drove around looking at the multiple formations of local rock. They chose a rock style that is similar in composition to Mary Colter's Grand Canyon designs, most notably the stonework at the base of the Watchtower at Desert View and at Lookout Studio. The snug placement of the multicolored, irregularly shaped boulders in both the interior and the exterior surfaces is an expression of dramatic strength, yet it imparts an unexpectedly sensitive and alluring presence. Inside, for example, the central design feature is the two-level kiva form clad in stone. Inside the kiva is Bob's office. It houses curving shelves, red rock door surrounds, and a radial-beamed skylight. Outside the kiva, a staircase to the guest rooms below clings to the rocks. The curving railing of wrought iron was designed by the architect Mike Bower and fabricated by Cottonwood artist David Platt. A stained-glass clerestory adjacent to the kiva is the work of Sedona glass artist Tom Aderhold.

Not only do the Pattersons enjoy the sensual comforts of their ideal interior spaces and their views of the Wilson Mountains, they enjoy the special pieces of sculpture that enliven their garden and the little bridge approach to their front entry. Iron, copper, and bronze sculptures against the stone backdrop of the house create a garden of delights among the rare and invaluable trees the Pattersons adore and strive to nourish. Sedona is lucky to have the Pattersons' roots growing here.

The stone cladding and round forms of the Patterson residence echo the composition of Mary Colter's Watchtower at Desert View.

ABOVE: *The bronze sculpture* Little Girl *by Joyce Killebrew and steel bridge by David Platt create a joyful approach to the home.*

OPPOSITE: *The views of Wilson Mountain are the focus of the windowed side of the house.*

LEFT: *A copper waterfall by David Platt graces the front entrance.*

CENTER: *The curved railing around the central kiva was designed by the architect Mike Bower and fabricated by David Platt.*

RIGHT: *Bob Patterson's home office is in the interior of the kiva and features a skylight.*

LEFT: *The radiating warmth of the central kiva is enhanced by the stained-glass clerestory. The glass is by Tom Aderhold, and the standing cheetah bronze is by Dutch artist Loet Vanderveen.*

RIGHT: *Open beams and curved walls accentuate the sensual interior furnishings by Jennifer Aderhold.*

FORMS OF MEXICO

architect: **CHARLES VAN BLOCK**

AROUND SEDONA, it is unusual to find a site that is *not* sloping into a creek or a canyon. This site, as Charlie van Block says, is better for building; the land does not slope as much, so one can "live more on the ground." Van Block approaches Mexican modernism with a strong attitude about emotional and intuitive space. He begins with the principle that Mexican architecture is about the walls, never the windows; about feeling nature most directly, rather than being removed from it, by, for example, a high "floating" deck. The walls are thought of as being sheltering and protective. They are rough-plastered and fused with huge, circular saw-cut beams, and heavy old wooden doors. From the outside, the forms are viewed as a series of cubes and rectangles. They are, on the inside, however, refined, intricate, and highly detailed as compositions for incoming light streams, a precious view, or clerestory illumination.

The owners themselves are design professionals who requested little architectural embellishment. Their familiarity with the work of the modern Mexican masters, including Luis Barragán and Ricardo Legorreta, who have been icons in

LEFT: *In the entry tower, the large square overhead window reflects Lizard Head Rock in the distance.*

OPPOSITE: *The paved courtyard entry is a sculpture of forms, niches, and materials that reveal little of what is on the other side of the facade.*

The orchestration of light and shade, texture and color is a changing gift to each visitor.

van Block's architectural pantheon since his childhood in Mexico, allowed the house to evolve from their many enjoyable conversations on art and design.

The spacious floor plan flows easily from one room to another. The design shapes itself around the existing irreplaceable trees on the site as well as the movement of the sun. Architecture in Sedona always welcomes the sun in winter and when successful, keeps it out in the summer. Views also drive the design: the tower entry is not simply to mark the entry in the usual manner of a "first impression." It has a purpose, in that it frames the striking Lizard Head Rock in the large high window that can be seen from the living room. In van Block designs, the results create physical comfort as well as the aesthetic and psychological pleasures associated with physical well-being.

Native stone was used, but just enough to establish an indigenous feel. The architect designed the covered porch as if its old walls, columns, and fireplace were restored from ruins from which the rest of the modern house grew. The owners suggested that the color of the main house come from studied samples of local red rock. Its strong, dark coloration makes this large house blend into the piñon, manzanita, and evergreens, becoming part of the landscape.

Lines and angles, volumes
and niches of the facade tell
the story of their own history
and their own art.

LEFT: *Space flows beside the living area, dining area, and master suite. The openness is a gallery for the owners' engaging collection of art.*

RIGHT: *The master suite with traditional open-beam ceilings is paired with classic Herman Miller pieces. The sunken private library is on the left.*

OPPOSITE: *The dining room is a skillful blend of Mexican craft in wood and African art. The exterior "room" was designed by the architect around an existing tree adjacent to the dining area.*

LEFT:
*The outdoor room is a signature
feature of the architect's love of
designing for sophisticated living
in the outdoors.*

OPPOSITE:
*With its infinity edge, the secluded
canyon basin swimming pool
seems to flow right into the
wilderness of the adjacent
National Forest.*

FERRYS' GARDEN

owners: **AIDEN AND LINDA FERRY**

architects: **DESIGN GROUP ARCHITECTS**

AFTER TWENTY-SEVEN YEARS of living in Chicago, the Ferry family was eager for a different landscape and particularly a different climate. They first visited Sedona in the late 1970s and found themselves drawn back more frequently in the years that followed. The red rock country finally lured them to Arizona, where they planned to build their new house. They knew at the beginning of the project that the main objective of the new design would be to capture every available view in as many rooms as possible. They worked closely with Design Group Architects and interior designer Jennifer Aderhold throughout the design process.

In Chicago, the Ferrys had lived in a Frank Lloyd Wright Prairie house. They were well acquainted with the feeling that comes from a house designed to "hug the landscape," in a horizontal design with an expanse of large windows. With this enormous opportunity to combine high style and energetic charm, the architects began with a long, horizontal plan featuring five vignettes under gently angled roof planes on an east-to-west grid. The exterior deck piers and chimneys were clad in the red rock horizontal pattern. The landscaping close to the house harmonizes well with the cladding and expanses of glass until the house dissolves into the landscape and its environs. The five-angled roof planes are the only indication that there is an element of artifice in the area.

Aiden and Linda Ferry were excited with the thought of designing a house in a climate where outdoor activities and space are as important to design as are interior spaces. Creating a warm, welcoming environment became the prevailing motif throughout the design phase.

The congenial air is first noticed in the interiors by the use of thin rock laid in a delicate horizontal pattern, occasionally broken by larger rocks on interior walls and fireplaces. The sense of informality, however, is greatly increased by the confluence of the main entry with the living room, dining room, kitchen-party area, and the exterior courtyard. Five prominent interior spaces have thirty-degree ceiling planes, which add height and emphasis to the overall open central floor plan. The glass and voluminous space in the adjoining central spaces promote the inviting garden atmosphere of the house. Soft colors and the texture of pine and birch woods used in many of the handcrafted pieces of furniture add to the softness of the spaces. The central hallway opens onto a garden terrace and courtyard lush with climbing vines, ornamental grasses, and a red rock water feature. The courtyard is visible from all of the main family rooms of the house and completes the Ferrys' home garden and their quest for freedom of space.

Three of the house's five roof planes define individual vignettes for living spaces inside.

ABOVE: *Handcrafted furnishings were designed by Jennifer Aderhold for the dining area. The open kitchen is across the hall.*

OPPOSITE: *The large living space is cozy with furnishings, fireplace, and fine art.*

*A rusted steel gate leads to
the enclosed patio garden.*

A sunken garden is surrounded by patios leading to the living room through either the main hall or kitchen

EL ROJO GRANDE RANCH

owners: **KARIN AND JIM OFFIELD**

architects: **DAVIS FREDRIKSON DAVIS ARCHITECTS**

EL ROJO GRANDE is a private ranch composed of the owner's residence, guest quarters, and ranch buildings. Colossal rock formations surround the heroic 140-acre site. The principal architect, Douglas Fredrikson, describes the architecture itself as an abstraction of the natural formations of red rock and the outcroppings that dominate the site, which are prevalent in the area surrounding Sedona. The ranch buildings, stables, riding arena, tack room, and barn are in the valley of the property. The residences overlook the valley from the rim rock above.

The centerpiece of the ranch is the principal residence, which is designed in a circular shape around a central kiva. The main entry, the kiva, is topped off by a rusted steel cone that acts as a solar chimney, drawing hot air up and out of the area when kiva doors and windows are opened. As a natural ventilation system, the cone roof generates and circulates cooler air, while providing shade for the courtyard. The interior spaces of the house are arranged around the circle of the kiva and follow the path of the sun during the day.

OPPOSITE: *A welcoming and leisurely entrance to the ranch introduces the design motif.*

RIGHT: *The Mesoamerican ziggurat motif pattern of the corral, combined with soft curves, can be found throughout the ranch.*

The focal point of the interior space is the great room, which features a large stone fireplace and windows that frame the red rock spire and formations towering above the ranch.

Sensitive building orientation and thick, bowl-shaped exterior walls shield vertical interior walls from heat. Fir trellises filter light and heat as well. Small buildings surround the main house: the pool cabana, spa, and a sunken fireplace. The overall sense is an open pavilion of outdoor patios that connect to the living spaces. Battered plaster walls, dry stacked sandstone walls, stained wood beams, and glass are featured inside and out for a continuous sense of outdoor living.

ABOVE: *The main entrance to the residence features a bold rusted steel cone canopy above a central kiva space*

OPPOSITE: *From the rim rock, the ranch below is sheltered in the valley.*

UPPER LEFT:
The interior of the kiva under the cone canopy.

UPPER RIGHT:
A room for guests with the scenic red rock buttes in the distance.

LEFT:
The guesthouse and patio in the evening light.

OPPOSITE:
In a room for casual get-togethers, the fireplace, piano, and bar create the perfect setting for entertaining.

ABOVE LEFT: *Corrals and stables down the slope.*

ABOVE RIGHT: *Beautifully curved, sloping stone walls are hollow, creating a cooling system between the exterior heat and the interior space.*

The equilibrium of landscape and architecture.

WESTERN QUARTERS

owners: PETER AND SUE BELLUSCHI

design team: RICHARD DRAYTON, CRAIG STEVENS, MICHAEL R. MCCULLOCH, AIA, ANTHONY C. BELLUSCHI, FAIA

AT ITS 4,500-FOOT ELEVATION, Sedona has historically been a day-trip from other parts of Arizona. In the mid-1970s, the small town served as a refuge from sultry temperatures and the wear of the desert to the south. It was the perfect place to spend mornings hiking the trails, playing tennis, meeting friends for entertainment, and discovering the latest galleries. Intrepid travelers, dedicated athletes, and ardent lovers of art and architecture, Sue and Peter Belluschi fell in love with Sedona during those day-trips on vacations to the Southwest. The cooler air in Sedona absorbs the incense of juniper and piñon. Whether translucent blue or thick with ambiguous tangerine-grizzled clouds, the sky and the red rocks form a kaleidoscopic backdrop to the drama of weather as it moves through the canyons. This was enough to convince them to build a house here.

Few can appreciate architecture in the way that Sue and Peter do. A family tradition gives them an uncommon perspective for the great architecture of the world. It prepared them for the stewardship of several timeless and treasured homes. Their elegance is simplicity and their joys include outdoor life as well as working with artists and architects with basic materials.

The design of their Sedona home was a collaboration of architects and artists, and of course, the owners. The lead designer, Richard Drayton, is a local Sedona artist who worked with Portland, Oregon, architect Mike McCullogh and Sedona furniture designer Craig Stevens. Peter also consulted his brother, Chicago architect Tony Belluschi for input and ideas. The construction began on an acre of land, below Cathedral Rock.

A major design feature in the house is the use of five-hundred-year-old Douglas fir. The old-growth timbers were salvaged from a seventy-year-old warehouse building in the Pacific Northwest. Peter meticulously selected each rough-hewn beam that was needed for the house and its furnishings.

Richard Drayton designed the house sited to the red rock. He used two complementary southwestern design themes: a classic joinery dovetail pattern and a Meso-american ziggurat design. Together they are the integral ornament of this contemporary dwelling. The dovetail is introduced at the front entry in the four-hundred-pound, four-plank Douglas fir door. The door is mounted in a frame that bears an insignia of its Wild West origins; a bullet embedded in a plank. The front entry of local stone opens into a spacious living and dining area. Designed for festive gatherings, the large kitchen space opens to the living and dining areas, with a bar-counter that insures everyone will be included in both the cooking and the festivities.

A western spin on modernism combines simple motifs, design, and the environment.

The compact design glows with the dignity of a desert treasure on the one-acre site.

The outdoor terrace almost touches the desert vegetation, with crystalline views of Cathedral Rock.

LEFT: *On the fireplace is a 1905 Marlin rifle, which was a gift to Peter Belluschi.*

BOTTOM LEFT: *The master bedroom, with patio and view.*

BOTTOM RIGHT: *The famous large Belluschi kitchen, with open counters on both sides and the dining area nearby. Furniture was designed by Craig Stevens.*

A curved local stone wall passes from the exterior walkway through glass panes into the living room. The ceramic pot is circa 1200.

LEFT: *The four-hundred-pound door was constructed from four planks of Douglas fir. The dovetail design is introduced at the front door and carried throughout the house. There is a bullet lodged in the door to the left of the handle in the second plank.*

RIGHT: *The outdoor sconce was created by Craig Stevens from hand-cut roof tiles.*

Five-hundred-year-old Douglas fir timbers were salvaged in the Northwest for structural use in the house and for the furniture.
Peter Belluschi selected each piece.

SOUTHWEST CRAFTSMAN

owners: **STEVE AND CONNIE SEGNER**

architects: **DESIGN GROUP ARCHITECTS**

PRIOR TO BUILDING this new home in Sedona, the owners had lived in Pasadena, California. During the many years they spent restoring homes in that area, they became devoted to the old-style homes and began collecting antique furnishings and Spanish lighting fixtures. When they started thinking of building in Sedona, their thoughts turned to true southwestern adobe. Along the way, their love for Spanish antiques evolved into a love of Arts and Crafts pieces. This was a natural fit for the Segners' home; the classic adobe building transforms itself with carved wooden features and ironwork associated with the Arts and Crafts style.

The materials the Segners wanted to live with were organic; the eighteen-inch-thick walls of the adobe structure were the perfect choice. The stylized craftsman doors tie the design together with a sophisticated simplicity. The interior of the house reflects a language of rusticity, simplicity, and craft. An exaggerated post and beam featured in the living room emphasizes the organic nature of the designs. Throughout the exterior, stone and beams form the groundwork of a lovely outdoor garden and courtyard, leading to a studio workshop and to guest quarters.

OPPOSITE: *The craftsman adobe blends with its setting.*

RIGHT: *Every detail reveals the owners' emphasis on craft and workmanship.*

Each detail of the Segner home is a tantalizing moment of sanctum. A small wood-frame window in the thick adobe wall; the balance of weight, color, and proportion of the gray stone and red rock chimney; the rusted curves of the iron gate, light fixtures, and fireplace screen; the large squares of terracotta tile along the hall of the *corrédor* to the studio all invite a lingering, fascinated glance. After the finishing touches were completed, the Segners couldn't give up their love of building; they went on to complete work on a twelve-room inn of the same style: El Portal Sedona.

ABOVE LEFT: *The multi-hued stones in the chimney were selected to balance the simplicity of the adobe.*

ABOVE RIGHT: *A wooden header over a tiny window is an elegant detail in the thick adobe walls.*

OPPOSITE: *A cool craftsman* corrédor *leads to the studio workshop*

UPPER LEFT:
*Beloved basset hounds
watch for visitors through the hand-
forged main gate.*

UPPER RIGHT:
*The guest quarters in
the shadow of the red rock.*

LOWER LEFT:
*The guest bedroom is
furnished with western craft pieces.*

LOWER RIGHT:
*Western art, stacked
rock, and fogon fireplace evoke the
atmosphere of the old West.*

OPPOSITE: *The living room
blends craftsman and adobe styles.
The wall curves to the form
of the large post under the beam.*

NATURE'S INN

owners: DOUGLAS EDWARD ANDREWS AND ROBIN ANDREWS

DOUG ANDREWS IS AN AVID hiker and explorer, as well as an artist. He is passionate about the wilderness and finds freedom in creating his own house and his own furniture as well as in painting the land and skyscapes of Arizona. Doug and his wife, Robin, share the treasure of their passions with their six-year-old daughter, many close friends, and collectors of Doug's work.

The inspiration for their house came from the couple's love for plants, horseshoes, and a certain Rocky Mountain cedar log measuring twenty feet by six inches. The standing vestige of it, with a thirty-eight-inch diameter, is the crux of the house, for it is the roof's center support. The exterior of the house sports a roof garden measuring fifty feet by thirty feet, which includes a full sod lawn with barbecue and horseshoe pits, flower gardens along the perimeter, and a lovely view of the lower lawns, nearby creek, and canyon.

The interior of the house is just as unique. A fish pond is next to the main entrance. It is surrounded by tropical plants, cacti, lily pads, vines, and ferns. A creek that runs through the property was the source of the massive rocks used in the pond and other parts of the construction.

OPPOSITE: *Doug has created a natural science museum for his daughter and her friends. This is their favorite place to visit. The central post of the Rocky Mountain cedar log is the inspiration for the evolution of the house.*

The view from the roof of Nature's Inn. This is a favorite place for horseshoes and barbecues.

The living area is the first level of the house; the kitchen, dining, gallery, and library areas are built around the pond. A rustic cedar staircase leads to a second-floor sleeping mezzanine. Down a colored glass walkway, past the peacocks, and through the trees is Doug's studio. There one finds the artifacts of inspiration and creation that have been collected on many hikes and explorations. For Doug, Robin, and their daughter, life in Sedona is a secluded paradise.

LEFT: *The Andrews' love of nature is evident when one of the morning peacocks roosts outside the kitchen window at breakfast time.*

CENTER: *Another of Doug's furniture creations is the kitchen table and collection of stools.*

RIGHT: *Doug's studio, where inspiration often comes during a game of pool. The reconstructed skeleton is made of elk bones found on hikes in the wilderness.*

Bathing can be a communal affair: family or peacocks may stop by

Nature's Inn is tucked deep into Oak Creek Canyon.

HOLISTIC HEARTH

owners: **JOAN TONYAN AND MARY HUDAK**

architect: **PAUL CATE**

JOAN TONYAN AND MARY HUDAK'S DREAM began about twenty-five years ago when they embarked on a holistic health pursuit of life. They lived in the Bay Area of California and traveled north to Columbia Gorge in Washington. Their search for a more ideal living environment eventually led to Sedona, away from the water and into the sunshine.

They were attracted by the healing energy they perceived to be housed within the majestic red rock formations of the Holy Cross Chapel area. There, after considerable feng shui observations, two major geopathic energy pathways were discovered on the site. It is believed that this retreat sits in the radiance of divine life-generating energy flows. Mary and Joan felt at once that this was the right place to support their spiritual goals for modeling a healthy plan and a teaching program in holistic health.

Mary and Joan also felt that it was fitting for the "birthing" of their house to design it with an organic integrity that expressed their respect for this bountiful setting. A rammed-earth construction was chosen for its ability to become an integral part of the beauty and energy of their surroundings.

LEFT: *The breezes dazzle the copper wind sculpture.*

OPPOSITE: *A stone path leads visitors into the entry courtyard.*

ABOVE: *The raw rammed-earth surface of the walls offers a sense of protection by the forces of Nature herself.*

RIGHT: *The raked rock meditation garden is a favorite place for cats.*

The house is sculpted from the red rock found on the building site. Its thick walls provide a steadfast buffer against the occasionally harsh outside elements. Large and expansive windows allow the sun to bring nourishment for body and soul inside the walls. Radiant in-floor heating during the winter months provides a gentle warmth throughout the house. The walls are conveniently thick for the creation of niches. The owners have also planted meditation, courtyard, and organic gardens. The gardens' harvest brings joy, peace, and food, reinforcing their beliefs that to teach and live in a healthy, organic, and energy-efficient environment is a meaningful adventure.

LEFT: *Rain water is captured in a stone basin.*

RIGHT: *Deep niches in the eighteen-inch-thick walls offer an ideal place to display and protect sacred objects.*

LEFT: *Artifacts in niches become a part of small altars.*

RIGHT: *A rain chain of tiny buckets.*

A private courtyard with red rock peaks overhead.

WEEKEND BESIDE OAK CREEK

owners: **BRIGGS AND BONNIE HUBBELL**

architect: **STEPHEN THOMPSON ARCHITECT**

BRIGGS AND BONNIE HUBBELL were looking for a weekend retreat "at the end of the road," and far from the buzz and glow of the city. One visit to the four-acre site on Oak Creek was all it took for them to realize they had found the refuge for their souls and the sanctuary from the world that consumed their everyday lives. It is a powerful and beautiful place, a part of their long-held dreams, and the opportunity of a lifetime. Pilgrimages to the property became their ritualistic escape even before the project was initiated.

Magnificent vistas, the uniqueness of the riparian desert oasis, the austere landscape, and the dark starry nights inspired a fundamental geometric form with exposed materials for the overall design. The outbuilding, or pavilion, vernacular of the area's ranching and farming legacy was the prototype form. The plan not only incorporated solar and wind orientations but also certain solstice and equinox axes that are of subtle importance to Briggs and Bonnie. These orientations are apparent in the layout of the site plan and highlight significant events throughout the year.

An earth-sheltered entry is reinforced with the incorporation of a bank vault handle. It is as much an experience to see the wheel (from an old tractor) turn and throw the bolts that free the wooden slab open as it is to be greeted with the creek-edge environment behind the home. Deep, shady patios protect the south and west glass while allowing the vistas to be viewed freely. Inside, a series of surprises waits around every corner. Attentive detailing and conscientious thought result in a cohesion and integrity throughout the home.

RIGHT: *Forms were borrowed from vernacular farm buildings.*

OPPOSITE: *The main entrance features a door handle from a bank vault.*

The vernacular architectural forms and materials combine with modern lines to create an attractive exterior and innovative interior spaces.

LEFT: *The living room features a central fireplace with a concrete mantel and surround.*

RIGHT: *The master suite is spacious and cool. Concrete blocks make solid partitions.*

owner: **ALDO ANDREOLI**

architect: **ALDO ANDREOLI**

SEDONA DOESN'T REMIND ANYONE of SoHo. Aldo Andreoli has been practicing architecture for the past ten years at Sanba, a design and development company he founded in New York. His specialties are loft designs and conversions in TriBeCa and condominiums on the Upper West Side. Sometime in the midst of that busyness, Aldo took a fateful trip to Sedona for meditation and relaxation. Inevitably, he found a parcel of land of "incredible peace," and began building his retreat.

The design of the Sedona house tempers Italian style, international chic, and a meditative desert life. A simple rectangular form is animated by a Romanesque tunnel-vaulted roof in copper. The selection of materials is the design equivalent of the oxidizing copper deposits found in the surrounding red rock formations. The roof's patina is transforming Aldo's house into a camouflage of color that will eventually blend into the distant landscape.

OPPOSITE: *From the pool is infinity.*

RIGHT: *Humor is the fanciful side of design.*

The long, slender vaulted roofline and its patina slowly merge into the landscape

The interior rooms utilize light, lines, and curves for an endless variety of shadow and shade. Patterns made by shutters and window treatments are like voices, allowing the rooms to speak to one another. A wall of glass on the south side transforms the sky's temperament into décor. An inanimate room doesn't exist in Aldo's house.

Recently, Aldo made a permanent move to his Sedona retreat. He has design and architecture projects underway in the desert. After moving, following the events in New York in September of 2001, this Italian fellow, who rides a sunflower-yellow Harley and has a heart for stillness, found a home in the desert.

A vaulted clerestory above the second-floor balcony offers an expansive view from the interior.

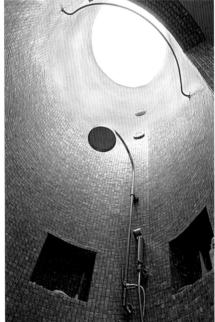

LEFT: *Soft tones, translucent shoji panels, hardwood floors, and an anthropomorphic mirror furnish a bedroom.*

CENTER: *Italian mosaic tiles are used throughout the large master bath, including the two-story skylighted shower.*

RIGHT: *An Italian twelve-drawer credenza.*

OPPOSITE: *The vaulted wood-paneled ceiling is linked to the hardwood floors by a wall of books and artifacts. The kitchen is adjacent to the living room; a hallway glides along the edge to the bedrooms.*

THE LIGHT HOUSE

owner: **SUZAN ANN MAGAZINER**

architect: **PAUL FRONCEK**

OF THE MANY ELEGANT HOUSES in Sedona that have been recently built or rebuilt, few possess the level of articulation found in the details of the Light House. Suzan Magaziner was looking for a feeling she described to her architect as "Southwestern Zen," a blending of cultural perspectives and spiritual traditions. The project was also an effort to create a three-dimensional sacred space as part of a journey for self-discovery, co-creation, recreation, and the full sensory embrace of beauty, magic, and substance. Suzan realized that vision as well as that of her architects. The project began with Sedona architect Charlie van Block, who initiated the design of the main room, covered porch, and kitchen spaces. The original post-and-beam work inspires the straightforward Asian feel as well as a sense of rhythm and order. For Charlie, "clarity makes a house peaceful," and this is what Suzan was looking for.

When East Coast architect Paul Froncek was introduced to the project, he and Suzan worked tirelessly to create and complete a sacred living space that is profound, but never overwhelming. Paul was introduced to the concept that architectural space is *always* a container for spiritual life, whether

The view through the foyer, double doors, and breezeway connecting the entry to the meditation room

it is recognized as such or not. From that introduction, Paul and Suzan focused on making the Light House an inspired assemblage of natural and handmade architectural elements along with significant, individual, energy-driven spaces. Suzan and Paul's creative work together influenced the formation of *Architectural Alchemy*, a spiritually based design collective. The goal of the collective is to teach that life is enriched through the design process and that architecture is a conduit for deepening spiritual commitments. The focus is to show that architecture is a source of ethical values. To create

OPPOSITE: *A pebble wall and fireplace are adjacent to a carved wooden door featuring a golden sun, an egg-shaped knob, and scrolls similar to sixth-century* mandorlas, *or halos of Japanese Buddha statues.*

sacred three-dimensional spaces, the collective espouses principles associated with stewardship, Power Feng Shui, geomancy, ancient dowsing, and technology. The Light House itself is a collection of many sacred spaces.

Power Feng Shui expert Valmai Howe-Elkins worked with Suzan and found the site to be a perfect location for a retreat and for healing. She noted how gravitational energy flows into the perfect bowl in which the house is placed, creating a protective "nest." The spaces in the house are so comforting and healing, reports Valmai, that at times it becomes very difficult to leave. The rooms are interspersed with courtyards, waterfalls, small meditation gardens, views, and pools. In addition to the divine architecture are the soothing guiding lights of carefully chosen interior objects. Part of taking an ethical stance in architecture involves an understanding of the sources and fabrication techniques of artifacts that are brought into the sacred space. For example, the Light House is furnished with handmade architectural essentials: egg-shaped lead door knobs, pebble stone walls, hammered tin lights from Asia, bamboo furniture, mosaic tulip fountains, handmade lanterns, and hand-carved doors and banisters. Each item is intended to inspire thoughtful examination of the item's place of origin, its impact on the community that produced it, and its positive generative power. Paul and Suzan are committed to sharing their process and their interior architectural resources through an avenue they call Sacred Doorways.

The house is tucked into a shallow bowl formation in the terrain

LEFT: *The living room with fireplace. There is a large crystal inside a capsule sunk into the hearth.*

RIGHT: *The master bath features a river rock wall, a pebble tub, and a faucet "rock" in the wall.*

OPPOSITE: *This warm, relaxed space features tin lanterns from India, salvaged timber posts and beam, and a country kitchen work table.*

*A handcrafted railing leads to the
pool, which is enriched by Suzan's
mosaic design and tulip fountains.*

LEFT: *The vestibule is an introduction to the peace found throughout the house. Feng shui artist Valmai Howe-Elkins suggested a dark blue to compress the available energy and open it into the large living room, where it could be contained and held. The carved double doors are Sacred Doorways.*

RIGHT: *There is a hidden water garden adjacent to the meditation room.*

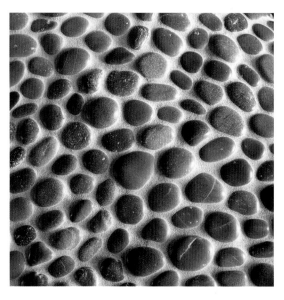

The crystal in the living room hearth is the source of all vital energy in the Light House.

A detail of the pebble wall.

One of the mosaic tulip fountains at the corners of the pool.

The hanging lounge with the landscape reflected in the glass. All materials are selected with a focus on the moral consequences and benefits of choice, materials, and production.

STONE OASIS

architects: **DESIGN GROUP ARCHITECTS**

IF THERE IS ONE HOUSE in Sedona that exemplifies a new indigenous architecture, it is this flawless design. While living in Osaka, Japan, the owners first read about the work of Design Group architects Max Licher and Mike Bower in *Architectural Digest*. Six years later they were searching the Four Corners area for a place to live. Driving south from Flagstaff they stopped in Sedona. There, they spotted a hotel magazine that featured another Design Group home, and the couple knew that these were the architects they wanted.

The owners wanted their home to be airy and welcoming with an elegant informality. The heavy lattice-patterned front gate opens into a round flagstone court, setting the tone. The entire floor plan is arranged around this central court, which is used for entertaining, dining, children's play, and poolside lounging. The owners are both triathletes who value outdoor life as a priority. Stone was also a primary consideration for the owners who wanted to *live with* it in their lives, and not simply view it as a facade. They wanted to feel embraced by stone, as if it were a "second skin." The family enjoys their total immersion into the design and the materials, and thrives on the complete integration of outdoor activities with interior spaces.

The front door to the house is inside the courtyard. Once opened, it reveals a dynamic arrangement of curves, stone, wood, light, and volumes. To the right of the front door is an attractive kitchen space defined by a curved counter that is adjacent to the living and dining areas. The three combined areas are separated from a lower level by a short staircase and a large glass aquarium wall featuring a perpetual ballet of tropical fish. A family room and bedrooms are below. To the left of the front door, a long, curved, interior glass hallway leads to a master bedroom, from which there is immediate access to the pool. Across the courtyard from the front door, stairs lead up to a small wing where the guest quarters and office are located. The overall design is compact and efficient. The views are extraordinary and framed as individual images at every opportunity.

The house is a masterpiece of composition and grace. The flat stonework and horizontal and vertical steel exteriors belong to the earth as naturally as any butte in the distance.

The door of the master bedroom opens to the lap pool.

LEFT: *The hall curves with the shape of the courtyard and leads to the master suite.*

RIGHT: *The kitchen and island are separated from the living area by a curvilinear counter.*
Overhead the volumes and clerestory increase the light and space.

The architects created a symphony with the music of textures, stone and steel, planes and curves.

The courtyard is a retreat surrounded by cool stone walls, warm timbers, and the swimming pool.

LEFT: *A large lattice gate opens into the courtyard.*

RIGHT: *Branches of the ocatillo against rust, steel, and red rock.*

LEFT: *This elegantly appointed living room features a round, stacked rock fireplace that is visible from the exterior.*

RIGHT: *A window over the aquarium frames the large red rock formation.*

OPPOSITE: *Steps lead down to a family room and sleeping wing. The aquarium set against a large peeled post is a window between levels.*

FULLER IS AN ARTIST and a descendant of twelve generations of New Englanders, who pulled up his historic roots and moved to Sedona when he met Jan, an ebullient public relations professional from San Francisco. Jan had discovered Sedona five years earlier in her quest for natural space and a more meaningful life. Now, married with two small children, they have discovered an old house with pioneer charm in a historic Sedona apple orchard. The 1948 red rock farmhouse was ready for a reclamation, and that is what this family had in mind. A drive through the orchard leads to the one-and-a-half acre property. There is room for Fuller's sculpture studio and plenty of open air in the orchard, where the children can play and are entertained by parents who build "pirate ships" that can be pulled through the trees by a tractor in search of "treasure." This eclectic life is filled with art, inspiration, and endless energy.

Fuller is a metal sculptor who creates steel artifacts. His creations include large and small furniture, lighting fixtures and sconces, geometric terrace and balcony balustrades, property gates, and freestanding sculptures such as the family dragon, "Major Drag."

The living room is designed to be reminiscent of an old fishing lodge, with a "Caught the Big One" steel fish mounted over the fireplace. An island made of steel palm trees, large rocks, and colorful tiles depicting sea creatures encloses an inner island that houses the kitchen stove. Poured concrete counters add dimension and color in the kitchen as well as to a bench that fits around the six-foot wooden table. Behind the concrete bench Jan and Fuller created a backdrop that is a nod to Frank Lloyd Wright's desert masonry. The original offset *saltillo* pavers, or handcrafted Mexican clay tiles, in the kitchen and living area were preserved in place. The walls were sandblasted and lightly stained to bring new life to the original knotty pine tongue-in-groove panels.

Every room is filled with niches, vignettes, steps, stairways, and doorways, all basking in the glow of Jan's color choices for wide, painted stripes and floral lighting. Views are carefully oriented to frame a select pine tree, distant mountains, fields of crops, and the apple orchard, creating a sense of nineteenth-century pristine red rock country.

Fuller's sculpture is an integral part of the house. The master bed and bath, the palm tree in the living area, and a tailgate guitar bench are part of the endless creative journey. Together, he, Jan, and their children continue to create a household that reflects the pure joy, happiness, and never-ending pleasure that they find in the creative aspects of daily existence.

The farmhouse, now fully restored, in the orchard. Major Drag, the family dragon created by Fuller, watches over all.

ABOVE: *The master bedroom is a collection of angles and windows. A partial wall shape separates a small workspace from the sleeping area. The bed was designed by Jan and Fuller and fabricated by Fuller.*

OPPOSITE: *A view of the living area with a large round table and "palm trees," by Fuller. A mosaic "seashore" washes up to the palms and boulders with tile starfish and crabs. The kitchen is on the right.*

LEFT: *The frescoed wall holds personal treasures.*

RIGHT: *The wall has a built-in niche for framed artifacts.*

OPPOSITE: *The house has built-in shelving and tables. A window separates bedroom and bath, and a corrugated column encloses bathroom fixtures.*

THE DRAGON FARM

owners: **VALMAI HOWE AND DAVID ELKINS**

THE OWNERS OF THE DRAGON FARM spent many years discovering, refurbishing, and bringing back to life several excellent old houses in the east. Valmai Howe is the high priestess of Sedona Power Feng Shui. She and her husband, writer David Elkins, moved to Sedona and miraculously found their way to an adobe cottage at the end of a long, winding, and bumpy road. They fell in love with the cottage and bought it and the property that abuts national forest land. The house was originally a studio built in the early 1980s, perfectly situated between a tree and a rock. Valmai and David honored the original intent of the first builder when they designed a recent expansion. The combination of the original adobe brick, straw bales, and red rock made the effort another hands-on experience for the owners, who invested their hearts and minds into the construction.

Valmai warmed the interior of the house with sun-baked colors and a *saltillo* tile floor, punctuated with deep blue deco tiles. Her love for a sensual environment is evident in her use of fabrics. Velvet fabric on furniture softens the room, as do velvet drapes tied with silk tassels. Tapestries and beaded silk lampshades add to the effect, as does the canopy over the bed. When the front door opens, the canyon breezes flow through a series of arches and circulate freely inside the house for an extraordinary daily refresher.

A carved wood door opens to the curve of the path and to a view of Augusta, the dragon.

Valmai and David named the Dragon Farm for the good fortune and creative energy attributed to the dragon in Chinese culture, a good fortune they have enjoyed ever since creating their new home. The rooms are designed as a refuge from the wild landscape of Sedona. Sedate and sublime, the protective folds in the surrounding canyon walls and hills are repeated in the undulating straw bale and native rock walls that enclose a series of imaginative outdoor courtyards. Near the pool is their heroine, a sculpture of the tranquil dragon Augusta. The flowing lines of the courtyards create a natural boundary for the pool. In the black, pebble-bottomed pool, there is also a rendition of Augusta. The pool was a *pet* project, designed by Tilke, the couple's daughter.

The undulating design and the softness of the interiors are only two of the features that make the Dragon Farm unique in its setting. The primary requirements for Valmai and David are comfort and privacy; a place to read, write, rest, and recharge. At sunrise and sunset, red-gold light flows over the property where walls and windows dissolve into the rocks and hills.

Augusta, cat, dog, and potbellied pig have a life of unfettered harmony and elegance. The Dragon Farm houses every bit of the charm and vitality that a lifetime of creating special places would have; it is simply a map of the energy and the patterns of the people living in it. One look at the Dragon Farm tells us that life is good.

Outdoor spaces are designed to reflect the curvatures in the rocks and hills. The pool and terraces ripple around the tiny footbridge and pergola, which houses Augusta. The flowing lines shape the pebble-bottomed pool.

The undulating stone wall and path are a complement to the prevailing winds.

ABOVE LEFT: *The Borzoi, Daria, relaxes in one of her favorite spots near the fireplace. Saltillo tile floors with blue deco drop-ins promise a casual and welcoming atmosphere.*

ABOVE RIGHT: *Dining chairs mimic the arched doorway to soften the space. The stone table gives the impression of foamy softness.*

OPPOSITE: *Foliage in the air and ciphers on the floor alter the perspective of the room.*

UPPER LEFT:

*An overhead canopy creates
an enclave for Mabel.*

UPPER RIGHT:

*Every room is a favorite
of Victoria's.*

LOWER LEFT:

*Air, light, and warmth
flow through the house.*

LOWER RIGHT:

*The kitchen is designed
for joy and efficiency.*

The pool and dragon nest at the base of the Forest Service land and wilderness area.

ART ASYLUM

owners: **JERRY AND ROXANNE FOLEY**

architect: **DALE ASPEVIG**

HAVING LEFT CHICAGO for worldwide adventure, the Foleys were inspired in every country they visited. But the small temples they discovered throughout Malaysia captured their spirits the most. The daily practice of stopping at a temple, removing one's shoes, and entering to offer an invocation appealed to them. What they found particularly pleasing was the nondenominationalism of the temples.

The spirit was with Roxanne when she and Jerry decided to live in Sedona. On a drive along an unnamed road that led to a smaller road, Roxanne saw an omen. In spite of a privacy sign, Roxanne wanted to stop; she walked around the sign, down the little red rock road, and over the hill where she found a "For Sale" sign on the property they had both been dreaming about. Their seven-and-a-half-acre desertscape has become their global retreat. In their distinctive setting, Jerry and Roxanne enjoy wildlife and the migratory birds. Goldfinches, orioles, bald eagles, and woodpeckers, as well as a variety of four-legged natives—elk, bobcat, fox, and coyote—live beside the Foleys in the one hundred acres of forest service land that borders their own.

RIGHT: *A sculpture signifies the Foleys' dedication to peace.*

OPPOSITE: The Maker of Peace, *a twenty-foot bronze Shaman sculpture by artist Bill Worrell, offers daily prayer.*

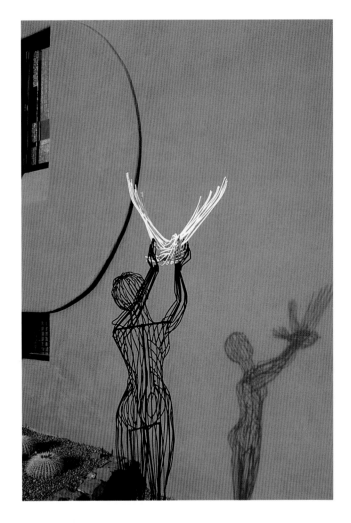

This small temple is the source of a discernible energy flow on the property.

The architect Dale Aspevig designed the house to fit into the hillside and suitably display the Foleys' extensive collection of art. The scope of the project changed dramatically midway through, when the Foleys discovered they would need a nursery, something not in the original plan. Aspevig reworked the plan and put the changes into place. The contemporary southwestern house is a great example of how to fuse the needs of indoor living and outdoor life. Boulders from the site trim terraces and pools. The architect worked closely with the artist in charge, Piero Resta, who carved two elegant old-growth timbers at the front entry entitled *Adam and Eve*. They rest on ball bearings and may be turned by hand in the manner of a Buddhist prayer wheel. A twenty-foot bronze shaman by Bill Worrell entitled *The Maker of Peace* blesses the land. The shaman is surrounded by standing Buddhas. On the summer solstice, across the wash from the main house, the sun sets in the center of the arch of a twelve-foot-tall ceramic sculpture. This sculpture, also by Piero Resta, was created and put in place even before the house was designed.

Adding to their symbols of earthly devotion, Jerry and Roxanne erected a small temple. Built of solid masonry, including a vaulted cast-in-place concrete ceiling, their chapel is inspired by the ancient temples of Crete. Moorish, Judeo-Christian, and Eastern religious symbols also influence building components. The three-quarter round arch doorway is painted in the alternating patterns and colors of the Madinar al-Zahra hall in Cordoba, in Muslim Spain. A stained-glass window reflects Navajo as well as Hebrew text. Christian crosses and Italian statuettes grace a low altar. A flow of spiritual energy that Roxanne describes as "palpable" enriches the air and the grounds.

The small, unnamed road that Roxanne recognized as an omen was a *roji*, a garden path that leaves the outside world behind and leads us to a newly created environment.

This twelve-foot-tall ceramic arch sculpture was created by artist Piero Resta and placed across the dry wash before the house was designed. The sun sets in the center of the arch on the summer solstice.

Sculpture is even more breathtaking at the edge of the water and wilderness.

LEFT: *A reflecting pool leads to Buddha and a standing stone sculpture by Piero Resta. Symbols carved into the stone are meant to recognize infinite and ancient energy.*

RIGHT: *A copper lotus flower fountain created by Piero Resta stands at the entrance. A "prayer wheel" carved post turns on ball bearings at the entry.*

Interior and exterior architecture form the divine temple of a pantheon, where images of and memorials to the gods are collected.

A view from inside the small chapel.

FIRE DANCER

owners: **PAMELA AND ANDREW KASKIW**

architects: **DESIGN GROUP ARCHITECTS**

AT 3,600 SQUARE FEET, this lovely Sedona southwestern Zen home satisfies its owners' desire for a sense of place and space. Sedona is small, and it is still difficult to find the right place to build. Eventually, the Kaskiws were led by Sedona's peculiar lure to the site they had been longing for. They visited their new property often, and on one of those visits, they watched "the colors of the sunset dance across the clouds, moving toward Cathedral Rock." That was when they decided to name their still unbuilt house "Fire Dancer."

Situated on an extremely steep site of almost solid rock, the house and decks have a commanding view of the valley and of Cathedral Rock formations in the distance. The house is an exquisite unfolding of cubes and cylindrical forms. The owners did not live in Arizona while the house was being built; they gave their complete confidence to the architects and to their builder. The Kaskiws' love of family, friends, and entertaining drove the design for their home, as is evident from the spacious kitchen, the media room, and the perfectly stocked wine cellar.

OPPOSITE: *One of many ornate niche altars in Fire Dancer.*

RIGHT: *The stone garden with rock sculpture and a Buddha.*

Sharing their love for sanctuary, the owners have also created a panoply of virtue with gardens, chapels, and altars. The largest chapel, consecrated as the Chapel of Divine Wisdom, is used for ordinations, classes, and visioning gatherings. Sacred energy is housed in the small chapel with its domed ceiling. The dome features a delicate ceiling fresco: a translucent lotus blossom encircled by symbols of the first seeds of Life.

Fire Dancer is filled with ceremonial niches and mantels dedicated to the artifacts the Kaskiws collected during their extensive world travels. Formal and informal altars covered with fresh flowers, candles, and offerings glow throughout the house and patio. Pamela and Andrew honor all religions and beliefs within their walls, under the blessing of Cathedral Rock.

Planes and circles of Anasazi and Asian influences
blend for perfect balance and style.

Fire Dancer cascades down the slope as a collection of volumes in stone, adobe, and mahogany.

UPPER LEFT:

The living room fireplace is surrounded by artifacts from the owners' world travels.

UPPER RIGHT:

The staircase has a niche altar between levels.

LEFT:

The Chapel of Divine Wisdom houses sacred energy under a dome and a fresco of a lotus blossom.

OPPOSITE:

The living room, bar, and dining area feature purple slate floor tiles and custom furnishings.

PERRY'S HILLTOP

owner: **LEIGH PERRY**

architect: **CHARLES VAN BLOCK**

SAVING TREES ON A SLOPING LOT isn't easy to do; nonetheless, architect Charlie van Block designed this house and saved two large, very nice piñon pines. Piñons take an extremely long time to get large, so when they do reach maturity, they are considered to be treasures in this part of the country. These two piñons embrace a large covered porch on the northwest side of the house. The porch is the anchor of the structure and inspires the feeling of being in a treehouse in the wilderness. This grand, expansive porch is the main space of the house; it has a dining area on one side and a sitting area and fireplace on the other. It is situated *just so* between the two large trees to frame the distant view of Thunder Mountain and its ridge of rocks that tumble down to Coffee Pot Rock and Devil's Kitchen.

The contractor asked if the porch could be built at a forty-five-degree angle, rather than the forty-six-degree angle shown on the plans. The architect double-checked and found that a one-degree shift would lose the framing of the main view, throw off dimensions for the length of the house, lose trees, and miss views entirely.

OPPOSITE: *On the expansive porch of this lovely hilltop home, the view is framed by the architect's signature detail of double posts.*

RIGHT: *A large wooden door opens into the quiet elegance of the entry.*

Early in the design process, the owner brought in feng shui consultant Valmai Howe-Elkins, who dowsed the land, reviewed the architect's drawings, and made her observations to her client. They carefully considered color schemes and a courtyard, which led to a few adjustments to the plan. Warm-hued tiles make up the floors throughout the interiors, with flagstone exterior floors in a variety of colors, including a peaceful sage green. Very few, but rather large, wood beams create a strong spatial and structural interior presence.

The house sits in harmony with its surroundings on the top of a hill, not unduly calling attention to itself; not causing a distraction from the rocks.

UPPER LEFT: *The courtyard sculpture offers a kaleidoscope of shapes and color; cloud formations and light are reflected in the glass.*

LOWER LEFT: *The central space is occupied by an open kitchen area with a gently curving cabinet counter.*

OPPOSITE: *The view beyond the dining room table.*

In the most remote landscape, symbolic art will be eternally recognizable.

Double posts enhance the magnificent views from the grand hilltop porch.

MARK RESIDENCE

owners: **ED AND MAURA MARK**

architect: **CHARLES VAN BLOCK**

THIS PARK CITY, UTAH, COUPLE married in Sedona. Life in Park City allowed them to make short getaways to the gorgeous red rock country in southern Utah, whose rock country is similar to the geology and climate of Sedona. But eventually their romantic origins caught up with them, and they found a spectacular site in the canyon lands of Sedona.

Ed and Maura have a love for modern design: simplicity, geometry, and spatial elegance. Large expanses of windows, cantilevered roof planes, large overhanging eaves, and crisp corners form the spatial qualities of quietude and sophistication. As one enters the living room, there is an alignment with the cliffs of Long Canyon. For the architect, the cliffs are a strong "fourth" wall of the room, attributing assurance and strength to the space. The dining room, kitchen, and family living area "pinwheel" around the main entrance. A long hallway punctuated by skylights, niches, and beams creates a rhythm that leads away from the central entrance to the yoga and meditation room and bedrooms. To the right of the front entrance is a south-facing sun and a garden hallway that leads to the pool area and master suite.

The architect describes the floor plan as a necklace of cubes and rectangles connected at odd angles. To cover the collection of shapes, a shed roof was constructed for each section and is its own simple structure, independent of the others. Proportion is a difficult component in the architecture of Sedona; it is dependent on intuition and on what is outside the window. In the dining area of the Mark house the architect worked with the client's request for sixteen-foot-high ceilings. The Wrightian framing along the sides of the window and the rock formation in the distance perfectly fill the window with an unalterable composition.

Maura is an interior designer and worked with the architect to select colors and finishes, as well as to design built-in furniture. Deep greens and purples cool the pool area; soft rusts and greens highlight the hallway of the niches. Red rock in a dry stack pattern makes up interior flower boxes and walls, and two-foot squares of buckskin sandstone are used as floor tiles.

The Mark home is made for entertainment and outdoor living. One favorite spot is the covered porch off the family room. The porch is built close to the branches of nearby trees, ideal for early evenings reading and enjoying the sounds, smells, and passing breezes of the Arizona canyon country.

The pool runs perpendicular to what the architect calls "the fourth wall": the cliffs of Long Canyon in the distance.

The circular approach to the courtyard gate. Guest quarters are on the upper left. The family room and living spaces are in the center.

LEFT: *A yoga and exercise room is adjacent to a small courtyard garden.*

RIGHT: *Bold architectural features such as an oversized front door, a large sculptural handle, and swinging pivot add strength to the design.*

UPPER LEFT:

*Dining room furnishings were selected by Maura
Mark. The Marks' request for sixteen-foot windows in the dining
area resulted in a precision-framing of rocks in the distance and
a Wrightian panel of horizontal glass planes on the right.*

UPPER RIGHT:

*A long hallway with niches and skylights leads to
the meditation and exercise room, bedrooms, and a utility space.*

LOWER LEFT:

Midcentury classics furnish the living area.

LEFT: *A composition of graceful Modernist furnishings.*

RIGHT: *A steel shield sculpture is highlighted by recessed neon light above the mantel.*

owners: **JIM AND KATHY PEASE**

architects: **DESIGN GROUP ARCHITECTS**

SOMETIMES THE ROAD to Sedona is a long and winding one. For Jim and Kathy Pease, it began when Jim was a young lad taking spring break pilgrimages to the dude ranches of Arizona. He was excited by the desert and loved the life of it. When he and Kathy married and had five children, the entire family began making the annual treks to dude ranches for vacations. They had lived in cold climates and considered a move to Santa Fe, but it wasn't until the late 1980s that the couple discovered Sedona and decided to make it home. Sedona won their hearts with its near-perfect climate, small-town feeling, and dedicated visual and performing arts community.

Jim and Kathy bought three acres on a hill with 240-degree views that include well-known landmarks: Cathedral Rock, Boynton Canyon, Secret Mountain. The house is situated at the "brow of the hill" and is landscaped with bushy, low-growing manzanita and juniper. The trees are situated just outside windows and glass walls. The floor plan wraps the

OPPOSITE: *The roof planes of the Pease residence skip over the tops of low-growing manzanita and young juniper at the "brow" of the hill, providing a 240-degree view of Boynton Canyon, Cathedral Rock, and Little Sugarloaf.*

RIGHT: *An elegant detail of light openings, smooth adobe, and rough stone surfaces.*

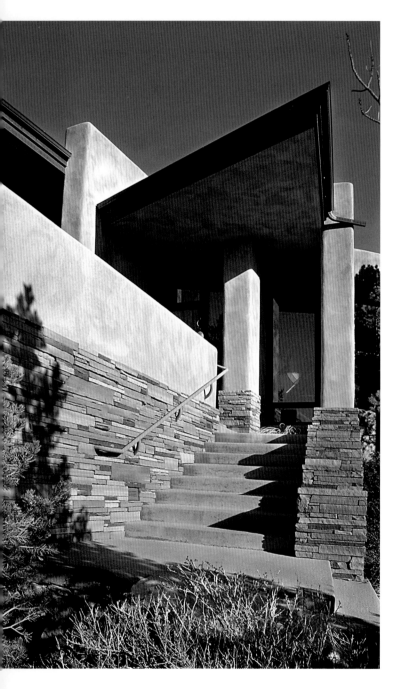

The front entrance features a stained glass wall designed by Tom Aderhold.

rooms around a circular courtyard. This elegant outdoor area features a red rock and sandstone waterfall, lush landscaping, and outdoor garden sculpture. The private garden offers a cozy, permeating desert sensation—a perfect counterbalance to the desert vistas in the distance. The plan radiates outward from the hillside courtyard garden.

The interior floor plan is designed for the enjoyment of the sights, whether of the courtyard or the vistas, from every room. Kathy and Jim's collection of Native American art, ceramics, paintings, and weavings are displayed on walls, atop pedestals made of layered stone, and along a softly curving half-wall ridge that overlooks the entry and leads to the north wing of the house. The kitchen, dining, and living rooms each have terraces and are adjacent to the courtyard. To the south of the main entry is an office, den, sleeping area, and Kathy's weaving room.

Kathy and Jim are patrons of the arts and showcase the work of local artists throughout their home. Kathy's own textile arts are masterful compositions of geometries, fractals, and color. The brave loveliness of her tapestries is a measure of one's ability to enjoy life. Kathy and Jim love the art and music that surround their daily lives, and enjoy sharing it with their children and frequent guests from the colder climes.

The weaver's room and spools of yarn. Kathy is a gifted weaver whose pieces are treasured tapestries of color and form.

LEFT: *The entrance to the living room is protected by a fanciful totem.*

RIGHT: *The foyer opens into a gallery and curved staircase, which leads to the main living quarters, weaving studio, and office.*

The view from the upper level over a half-wall to the main entrance.

A small terrace and sculpture garden off the hallway that wraps around the courtyard.

A path leads through stone walls and juniper, and past a freestanding steel sculpture installed in the landscape.

STILL TIME

owners: **HOWARD AND TRINA FELDMAN**

architects: **DESIGN GROUP ARCHITECTS**

IT TAKES TIME to get used to the redness of the earth, the stain of the cliffs, rocks, stones, and gravel that are Sedona. On a trip to Palatki, the ancient Sinagua ruins near Sedona, a crushed red rock path leads through a small grove of trees, up the slope of a red cliff, and trails beside the beautifully collapsing remnants and still-stacked red rock walls that blur into the enormous cliff face of the landscape. The approach to the Feldman house brings about a similar sense of anticipation and marvel. Here, though, the flat stones are precisely aligned. They form angles and curves. They are of varying thickness and color. They are, we know from Palatki, enduring. And more than that, they are infinite salvation to the eye and the creative spirit.

The design was a collaborated dream between the Feldmans, who bought the site in 1979, and Max Licher and Mike Bower of Design Group. The Feldmans wanted a house filled with natural light as well as one that would be "grounded," stepping down the topography of the landscape. Howard and Trina also expected a spectacular and provocative design. Once the design discussions were over, the architects were left with directions to design a home with an organic presence, yet clean-lined, with the high-strung sophistication of a metropolis. This might be a problem for any architect. However, in that typical Sedona manner, the concept revealed

itself to Max while he was on a hike. Max loves unusual rocks. He picked up one from a trail; the rock had several protruding crystalline forms jutting outward along one side. Nature again supplies the concept.

Access to the house reveals an extraordinary assemblage of stone surfaces: partial walls that appear as folded screens, full walls, and stepped walls of varying heights. Curved and angled surfaces of thin, horizontal, delicately layered stone lead to a series of steps to massive alderwood double doors. The doors are inlaid with steel plate in an abstract geometric form. To the left of the door, water falls over stacked glass into a shallow pool. A channel of water encircles the perimeter of the outside entry. Small windows are visible, but the overall impression is one of impregnability.

On the other side of the front door the world changes: stone is left behind, ahead stands the great emblem of modernity— glass. Five striking floor-to-ceiling ninety-degree glass bays span the north side of the structure and reveal nothing more than virgin land stretching as far as the eye can see. The great room, living area, dining area, reading area, and kitchen have four views of eternity. The fifth bay is in the master bedroom. Privacy is the key, and this design guarantees personal views of piñon pine, red rock, blue sky, and an occasional storm cloud.

A collaboration between the owners and architects resulted in architecture so astounding that to view it causes a "euphoria of experience." The pool of water and stacked glass waterfall at the entrance to the Feldman residence are symbols of meaningful advances in architecture. The curving, stepped-down roofline eventually dissolves into the mesa in the distance.

LEFT: *A narrow glimpse of the low, broad sweep of the main entrance at the top of the stone stairway reveals nothing of the present.*

RIGHT: *The interior reveals that the opposite wall of the residence is all glass and follows a natural ridge on the site. All interior spaces are oriented in this direction.*

A steel plate ornament with an abstraction of an ancient form is inlaid into the alderwood doors.
To the right the glass protrusion is the first hint of modernism.

LEFT: *The interior entry hall reveals the seed of the geometries that guided the design of the residence. It is based on the concept of the Golden Section, a roughly five-to-eight ratio, which Renaissance architects believed was divine. This concept is implemented in the entrance ceiling, which symbolizes water, fire, air, and earth.*

RIGHT: *The glass bays project onto the terraces and mimic the angular crystal forms Mike Licher found on a hike.*

OPPOSITE: *Watching the magic of the night sky from the privacy of one's home is a luxury for which there is always time.*

CONCLUSION

There is always one place whose architecture tells the story of the land. The architectural legacy of Sedona cannot be discussed without mention of the Sky Mountain home of Paul Schweikher. The structure is now lost, demolished to make way for ambitions that cannot match the integrity of Schweikher's moral aesthetic—what Eugène Emmanuel Viollet-le-Duc saw as the essence of true architecture.

If there is hope in the world for architecture to influence how we respect a place, projects such as Sky Mountain, even in their absence, cannot be ignored. It is a matter of honor, and in it lives our future.

THE SCHWEIKHER HOUSE ON SKY MOUNTAIN

owners: **PAUL AND DOROTHY SCHWEIKHER**

architect: **PAUL SCHWEIKHER**

PAUL SCHWEIKHER BEGAN his architectural practice in Chicago in 1928 and is widely admired for his post–Prairie School residential designs. He didn't believe in a philosophy of architecture; for that matter, he didn't believe in *having* a style. The old dictum, "life is stronger than design," always wins, and Schweikher knew he could count on that. It may be that he was a man far too subtle for fame as an architect— lacking the flair of Mies van der Rohe or Frank Lloyd Wright. However subtle he may have been, his designs were heart-stoppers; especially his classic Sedona residence.

Schweikher began designing a Sedona retreat for himself and his wife in 1970. He worked through five series of early drawings. The series of sketches did, finally, push him toward this masterly achievement.

The top of one of Sedona's many buttes offers a 360-degree view of the distant aeries. The house was designed to hover over large interior spaces arranged under one 105-foot unbroken roofline. Schweikher's fondness for the simplicity of vernacular barn shapes of the Chicago countryside, and the large open spaces common in Native

American long houses, influenced the shape and the deep overhanging eaves of the Sedona house. The wide overhang of the roof kept the glass walls hidden in shadow. What Schweikher did under the roof and eaves was brilliant. There is a bridge, a catwalk, a gazebo canopy, living space, a studio, a breezeway, a twenty-four-foot-long galley kitchen with a three-foot-wide plank, a dining area, and more—in a house with only three interior doors.

Schweikher's travels to Japan in 1937 influenced his use of spatial geometries in design. He utilized the geometric order, meditative aesthetics, and vernacular styling as seen in the repetition of patterning inside and out, as well as in the raked gravel in the courtyard and the drive. He loved the country trough–styled sinks and designed a simple maple and marble version for the bath. Also, he styled a stronger variation of shoji screens to accommodate privacy. All of these elements were orchestrated for an exceptional and functional residence.

Ironically, Schweikher didn't use the indigenous materials in the structure that are found in other Sedona designs. He capped his mountain retreat with a corrugated metal roof, one that he later decided wasn't quite right. What he did create however, was a new vernacular for the Southwest: one that emphasizes lyrical space in southwestern and Asian austerity. Because of its unparalleled attractiveness, Sedona must gain an architectural anchor-

The breezeway under the 105-foot continuous roofline offered a perfect view of Cathedral Rock.

ing and an accounting of an implied moral aesthetic. This is exactly what our friend Eugène-Emmanuel Viollet-le-Duc implied is the essence of architecture, at the beginning of our journey through this book. It *is* important. The Schweikher project teaches us about integrity, sensibility, and direction in architecture. It shows a future where architecture can exert its ethical influences, and where projects such as this one, even in its absence, will not be overlooked. Its absence? Sadly, the Schweikher house on Sky Mountain was demolished.

The legacy of Sedona is, "find your own stone." Paul Schweikher did.

The broad, low overhangs created a cooling system for the air as it passed through the shaded areas and around the corners of the residence.

The subtle design was patterned after farm and vernacular building styles of early Arizona communities.
The broad barn roof hovered to protect the very peak of Sky Mountain.

Like the freestanding Anasazi ruins, the Schweikher residence at Sky Mountain presented its simple form.

Schweikher adapted Japanese barn troughs for conventional use in marble and stone at Sky Mountain.

LEFT: *The upper-floor bedroom had a bridge leading to a loft.*

RIGHT: *The dominant design feature of the first-floor living area was a thirty-six-inch steel pipe that was used as a fireplace and ascended through the second floor. The steel plate that was cut out for the fireplace opening was installed as the chimney damper.*

The simplest needs require the simplest forms.

NOTES

1. V. B. Price, *Anasazi Architecture and American Design* (Albuquerque: University of New Mexico Press, 1997), p. 228.

2. Mary Austin, *The Land of Little Rain* (New York: Houghton Mifflin, 1903), p. 1.

3. Ibid., p. 6.

4. John Van Dyke, *The Desert* (Gibbs-Smith: 1980), p. 200.

5. Ibid., p. 56.

6. Bruce Brooks Pfeiffer, ed., *Frank Lloyd Wright, Collected Writings, Volume 4, 1939–1949* (New York: Rizzoli International Publications, Inc., in association with the Frank Lloyd Wright Association, 1994) p. 35.

7. Arata Isozaki, *Frank Lloyd Wright: Johnson and Son, Administration Building*, Global Architecture I (Tokyo: A.D.A. EDIT, 1970), p. 2.

8. Quoted in Ezra Stoller, *Frank Lloyd Wright's Taliesin West* (New York: Princeton Architectural Press, 1999), p. 7.

9. Bruce Brooks Pfeiffer, ed., *Frank Lloyd Wright, Collected Writings, Volume 4, 1939–1949* (New York: Rizzoli International Publications, Inc., in association with the Frank Lloyd Wright Association, 1994) p. 170.

10. Ibid, p. 36.

11. Arnold Berke, *Mary Colter, Architect of the Southwest* (New York: Princeton Architectural Press, 2002), p. 7.

12. Ibid. p. 307, fn. 53.

13. Dorothea Tanning, *Between Lives: An Artist and Her World* (New York: W. W. Norton and Company, 2001), p. 141.

14. Ibid., p. 155.

15. Ibid., p. 145.

CREDITS

Bell Rock at dawn.